BUILD A BETTER US

A BETTER

HIM

31 DAILY CHALLENGES

FOR MEN TO LOVE GOD, THEMSELVES & OTHERS BETTER

BJ THOMPSON

Written by **Vanja & BJ Thompson**

Edited by **Danielle Anderson**

Cover & Interior design by **Melissa Webster**

Interior Format & Layout by **Melissa Webster**

31DAYGROWTHCHALLENGE.COM

And he said to him, "You shall love the Lord your God with all your heart and with all your soul and with all your mind. This is the great and first commandment. And a second is like it: You shall love your neighbor as yourself."

MATTHEW 22:37-39

TABLE OF CONTENTS

OUR LETTER TO YOU

If we're honest, we can all do better in the areas of faith, relationships, and self-care. Growth in these essential areas won't happen magically, it requires that you and I are proactive and intentional about developing habits that lead to meaningful transformation. I can personally attest to passively waiting for growth to happen in relationships, personal care, and faith, only to realize I was grossly immature. I had to decide to stop making excuses, create habits, and stick to a regimen that led to a better me.

A Better Him is a 31-day challenge that lays out simple ways to create meaningful health in these critical areas. Based on the biblical call to "Love God, Love yourself, and Love others," this resource is meant to give the reader simple yet effective practices that bring life to your faith, relationships, and self-care. It's not a magic formula for growth, but rather a set of daily exercises meant to encourage growth in each area. Like any challenge or training, whatever you put in is what you'll get out. Take these challenges seriously, and you'll see serious results. Take these challenges minimally, and you'll see minimal results. The 31-day growth challenge is for all people no matter your status, but if necessary, feel free to modify any challenge so that it better fits your unique situation, time restraints, or context.

NOW, LET'S GET STARTED!!!

Dear Lord,

I pray that you give this man courage to relinquish control and pursue a level of uncomfortable growth that makes your grace evident. Give him deep joy, increased love, and a re-energized soul. I pray for restored relationships, tangible charity towards others, and self-reflection that leads to life transformation and a new trajectory. I pray for deep and rich experiences that create lasting memories with others, himself, and You.

IN JESUS' NAME, AMEN.

GETTING THE MOST OUT OF THIS BOOK

The challenges in this book are organized under three pillars—**Faith, Others, Self-care**—representing the three distinct areas of intentional growth. It is up to you to determine the order in which you will complete the pillars, but once you've started a pillar, please complete the challenges within that specific pillar in the order prescribed.

For example, you may choose to complete the pillars in this order—Faith, Self-Care, Others. If so, here is what your 31-day journey would look like:

> **FAITH:** DAYS 1-10
> **SELF-CARE:** DAYS 11-21
> **OTHERS:** DAYS 22-31

If you choose to complete the pillars in this order—Self-Care, Others, Faith—here is what your 31-day journey would look like:

> **SELF-CARE:** DAYS 1-11
> **OTHERS:** DAYS 12-21
> **FAITH:** DAYS 22-31

HERE ARE A FEW RULES TO HELP YOU GET THE MOST OUT OF THIS 31-DAY CHALLENGE:

(1) Limit your social media use to 30 minutes a day. In place of social media usage, practice the challenges, be present in your relationships, and be okay with spending time in silence and solitude so that you might get to know yourself.

(2) Daily journal your experiences, feelings, and revelations.

(3) Take this challenge with one other person or designate an accountability partner with whom you can process your experiences.

The goal of this 31-day challenge is to help you become more intentional and present in the areas of life that matter most. If you miss a day (or days), be gracious with yourself and catch up as soon as you are able. Remember, the more consistent you are, the more you'll see the benefits of the challenges.

HERE IS WHAT YOU CAN EXPECT TO SEE IN EACH DAILY CHALLENGE:

- *Cost to You icons* - these help you better grasp the time and financial commitment of the challenge.

$$\boxed{\frac{30}{\text{MIN}}}$$ = 30 MINUTES

$$\boxed{\frac{24}{\text{HRS}}}$$ = CHALLENGE LASTS 24 HOURS

$$\boxed{\frac{10}{\$}}$$ = $10.00

- *Personal story* - a short story from our own lives that will help illustrate the lesson
- *Truth* - a brief statement capturing that day's fundamental idea
- *Challenge* - the prescribed action for that day
- *Reflection* - Emotions, thoughts, & actions experienced?

Following each daily challenge there is designated space for you to journal. Ask yourself key questions and write your responses. What did you feel? What did you experience? What were some new thoughts?

PICK ONE

$$\boxed{\frac{30}{\text{MIN}}}\,x10$$

Do your best to present
yourself to God as one
approved, a worker who
has no need to be ashamed,
rightly handling the word
of truth.
2 Timothy 2:15

The word of God is more than a book; it's the active, living word of the divine Creator, spoken to all mankind. If I'm honest, it's easy to say, "the Bible contains important truths for my life." But it is hard to practice a routine of consistent study and reflection that would enable me to apply those truths. I've realized that when I fail to create an intentional time to read and study scripture, it never becomes a consistent practice in my life.

TRUTH INSIGHT

A person that prioritizes the regular reading, study, and application of scripture, is a person with keys to divine intelligence and guidance.

CHALLENGE

Today, identify a book of the Bible, with five chapters or less, to study. For the next 2 weeks, read and reflect on 1 chapter every day for 15-30 minutes. This can be a book relevant to your season of life or a book you've never read or studied before. Here are some helpful questions to ask yourself as you read:

(1) What's the historical background of the book?

(2) Given the historical background and geography, how would the people of that time have understood the words of the author?

(3) What are the timeless truths people today can learn from this book or passage?

(4) How does this relate to your personal life?

REFLECTION

_____

_____

_____

_____

_____

_____

_____

_____

_____

_____

_____

_____

_____

_____

_____

_____

_____

_____

_____

_____

_____

_____

_____

_____

_____

_____

_____

_____

_____

_____

SHAME THE DEVIL

30
MIN

Submit yourselves therefore to God. Resist the devil, and he will flee from you.
James 4:7

Have you ever been at a networking event and noticed, later, that you had a little green visitor hanging around in your nose? Your mind starts spinning, and you realize that in all those conversations not ONE SINGLE PERSON said, "Hey, you have something in your nose." Questions swirl through your mind. *Were those smiles genuine, or were they smirks because you had the green goblin dancing in your nose hairs?* All of a sudden you feel embarrassment, guilt, and maybe even shame, because you carried the nostril hulk around all night long, and no one said a word. It's a silly example, but the truth is far from silly. Shame and guilt are two of the greatest killers of our connection to God and others. Sadly, many of us carry shame and guilt from present and past actions. But if we truly desire to live with more freedom, we must first be honest about the guilt we're carrying. A famous quote says, "You cannot heal what you're unwilling to reveal."

TRUTH INSIGHT

Until you're willing to release shame and guilt, you cannot experience the freedom that comes from grace.

CHALLENGE

Today, write out a list of past and present things that have made you feel shame, and spend time confessing and releasing them to God. If necessary, call someone who's connected to your shame and apologize.

REFLECTION

_____

_____

_____

_____

_____

_____

_____

_____

_____

_____

_____

_____

GENEROSITY

But when you give to the needy, do not let your left hand know what your right hand is doing, so that your giving may be in secret. And your Father who sees in secret will reward you.
Matthew 6:3-4

Growing up, I believed that giving was something you did if people could pay you back later. (I know I'm not the only one who shared a few Skittles and expected an entire pack in return.) I realized that giving only to be paid back, or not giving because of skepticism of how a gift would be used, was depriving me of a treasure that, as the scriptures say, "moth or rust could not destroy."

TRUTH INSIGHT

Giving generously reminds us that God, not money, has the real power. It also reminds us that what we have doesn't ultimately belong to us, but it belongs to God.

CHALLENGE

Today, choose a public charity or organization whose work you'd like to see expanded in the world and make a donation. It doesn't matter the amount, but it has to be monetary.

REFLECTION

_____

_____

_____

_____

_____

_____

_____

_____

_____

_____

_____

_____

_____

_____

_____

_____

_____

_____

_____

_____

_____

_____

_____

_____

_____

_____

_____

_____

_____

_____

_____

_____

_____

_____

_____

_____

_____

_____

CRYING OUT

I will praise the name of God with a song; I will magnify him with thanksgiving.
Psalm 69:30

Growing up, I heard over and over that men don't cry. And when you hear a phrase so many times, from countless sources, you stop questioning whether or not it's flawed in any way. It wasn't until I married my wife that I realized relationships require a serious vulnerability that I had never attempted. I'd embraced the idea that "men don't cry" so seriously that when my wife needed me to be vulnerable, all I could do was shrug my shoulders. If it's true that for a healthy relationship to flourish you must learn vulnerability, the same has to be true for our relationship with our Heavenly Father. Do you struggle with vulnerability? No worries. Anyone willing can learn how to be vulnerable and, with practice, grow a deep connection with others.

TRUTH INSIGHT
Vulnerability is the fuel that creates a deep connection, but it requires that we understand and practice authentic vulnerability.

CHALLENGE

Today, carve out 30 minutes to practice vulnerability with God by worshiping Him through song (phone on airplane mode). Feel free to sing loudly, raise your arms, clap, weep, or whatever else you feel compelled to do.

REFLECTION

_____

_____

_____

_____

_____

_____

_____

_____

_____

_____

_____

_____

_____

_____

_____

_____

_____

_____

_____

_____

_____

_____

_____

_____

_____

_____

_____

_____

_____

_____

_____

_____

_____

_____

_____

PRAYER DATE

30	30
MIN	MIN

...pray without ceasing...
1 Thessalonians 5:17

Often times we treat prayer like a duty, but doing so perpetuates a transactional experience with our Creator - it doesn't inspire a deeper relationship. If you're like me, you can have conversations with people for more than an hour because there's a back and forth dialogue. If prayer feels scary, it may be because we don't have an informed understanding of the person we're dialoguing with. If that's the case, read through a short book of the Bible, or a Psalm, and pray those verses back to God. Through this practice we not only can grow in divine intelligence, but we also can grow deeper in our relationship. We get to be orderly and specific with each petition, but vulnerable as well.

TRUTH INSIGHT

Prayer unlocks divine wisdom and strengthens our inner being in unspoken ways.

CHALLENGE

Today, schedule time on your calendar to have a one-hour conversation with God. Before this time, write a list of praise, concerns, areas in which you need help, issues with family, or things that need to change in the world. During your conversation, turn your phone off. Feel free to keep your eyes open and just talk with God.

REFLECTION

_____

_____

_____

_____

_____

_____

_____

_____

_____

_____

_____

_____

_____

FASTING

24
HRS

*But when you fast, anoint
your head and wash your face,
that your fasting may not be
seen by others but by your
Father who is in secret. And
your Father who sees in secret
will reward you.
Matthew 6:17-18*

Fasting is an interesting subject. Many people have only fasted because they accidentally missed a meal. Others say they would fast but don't follow through just because they don't understand the importance of fasting. I've heard it said, "You are a soul with a body, not a body with a soul." This demands that we do things that strengthen our soul. One way to strengthen our souls is to fast. Fasting helps us acknowledge that our soul needs to be strengthened, just like our physical body. When we are hungry, we're reminded that our outer person, our body, needs to eat. But when we fast from food and intentionally deny our body, we are reminded of a divine power source that we rarely tap into. As a result, we learn how to experience and rely on divine strength.

TRUTH INSIGHT

Fasting reminds us that, to truly experience life, we need more than food, we need our Creator.

CHALLENGE

Today, plan to go 24 hours with no food and no sugary drinks - water only. It's not going to be easy, but it will be worth it. When you feel hungry, pray and ask for more divine power. Also, don't feel the need to announce that you're fasting, so that you can experience greater rearward. (If you have any pre-existing medical conditions or are under medical care, consult your doctor before completing this challenge.)

REFLECTION

_____

_____

_____

_____

_____

_____

_____

_____

_____

_____

_____

MANY MEMBERS

30	30
MIN	MIN

For just as the body is one and has many members, and all the members of the body, though many, are one body, so it is with Christ.
1 Corinthians 12:12

As a proud graduate of Lincoln High School in Dallas, Texas, you couldn't tell me it wasn't the best high school in the state or even the nation. It, of course, had its issues, but overall I firmly believed that no school could compare to mine. And, following that logic, I thought that no other student could equate to a student from Lincoln High. It wasn't until I got to college and became friends with students that had graduated from other schools across the nation, that I realized my comparisons were close-minded. Everyone had something valuable to offer, despite not having gone to Lincoln High School. I developed diverse friendships with some of those students, and that helped me see that good could occur outside of my small circle - my tribe. Sometimes a zeal for a denomination, theological stances, and cultural experiences, leads us to believe that the only good happening is within our tribe, but building friendships and having diverse experiences help us see and affirm the good outside.

TRUTH INSIGHT

God is and always has been at work doing good outside of our knowledge, experience, and tribe.

CHALLENGE

Today, think of a small group or church you've been curious about or invited to but never visited. Over the next 7 days, plan to attend and take note of the good happening in the service. Spend time praising God for the good you saw and experienced.

REFLECTION

_____

_____

_____

_____

_____

_____

_____

_____

_____

_____

_____

_____

MEMORY

30	30
MIN	MIN

*I have stored up your word
in my heart, that I might
not sin against you.
Psalm 119:11*

I have a terrible memory for details, as my wife often reminds
me. It's not that the details don't matter, it's that I'm so busy
with other more substantial efforts that it's hard to keep up with
what seems so small. But some "seemingly small" things have
a significant impact on what they are connected to. Have you
ever seen the size of a ship rudder? In comparison to the ship,
it's tiny, yet it sets the direction either into calm waters or into
chaos. Memorizing scripture is similar. Committing scripture
to memory seems small, but it's the difference between steering
into that which brings death or life to your soul. It allows us to
discern and make sense of life using God's eternal truth, not just
our feelings.

TRUTH INSIGHT

Those who hide scripture deep in their heart possess a weapon
that combats the ever-present schemes of Satan.

CHALLENGE

Today, look through your bible for 1-3 truths you need to remember about God's character. Write them on sticky notes and place them where you can see them easily so that you will regularly be reminded of God's truth.

REFLECTION

_____

_____

_____

_____

_____

_____

_____

_____

_____

_____

_____

_____

_____

_____

_____

WHERE ARE YOU?

"*Self-evaluation and assessment should be a major part of our lives as believers.*"
- *Sunday Adelaja*

As a free-spirited person, there is nothing worse than hearing my supervisor say, "Let's meet for our quarterly evaluation." I still cringe thinking about the many times in the past I've sat across from a supervisor as they evaluated every aspect of my work performance. Whose cruel idea was this? As much as I despise these evaluations with my boss, I've realized that without proper assessment, essential areas of life can go unattended for years at a time. Sadly, it often takes a major crisis for us to see the need to invest in a particular area. This is undoubtedly true of our faith.

TRUTH INSIGHT

Sober reflection and regular tending to our faith allow us to experience the abundant life our Creator intended.

CHALLENGE

Today, evaluate your faith. Write down your answers to the
following questions: How would you describe where you are
currently? What are the strengths/weaknesses? Where would you
like to be? What changes need to occur for your faith to grow?
When you're done, share your evaluation findings with your
accountability partner.

REFLECTION

_____

_____

_____

_____

_____

_____

_____

_____

_____

_____

_____

_____

_____

I'VE LEARNED

30	30
MIN	MIN

...and what you have heard from me in the presence of many witnesses entrust to faithful men, who will be able to teach others also.
2 Timothy 2:2

Have you ever taken a class or course for an entire semester and by the end, couldn't recall a single thing you learned? (Sadly I've done this more times than I'm willing to admit publicly.) Maybe the presentation of the material didn't connect, the information was irrelevant, or you didn't pay out-of-pocket for the course, so you literally were not invested in the class. Information only has an impact to the degree that we can recall, observe, and experience its implications in real life. Too often, people of faith go entire seasons of "learning" truth about God but, once the season is over, can't recall significant details. I'm growing in the habit of reteaching what I have learned. It forces me to own the information and think through it from varying perspectives. Teaching someone else what I have been studying in scripture has proven to be a fruitful exercise.

TRUTH INSIGHT

The degree in which we learn the truths of God is the degree to which divine intelligence and power are at our disposal.

CHALLENGE

Today, contact a friend, mentee, or co-worker and ask permission to schedule a time to reteach what you've been learning in this book study.

REFLECTION

_____

_____

_____

_____

_____

_____

_____

_____

_____

_____

_____

_____

_____

_____

MICROSCOPE

"Prioritize self-care and incorporate a MINIMUM of 60 minutes 'ME TIME' into your daily routine. YES, THERE ARE enough hours in the day. NO EXCUSES."
- Miya Yamanouchi

Growing up, I have vivid memories of my father working outside under his car. He would do everything: change the oil, replace critical parts in the engine, and more. And though I'd spent countless hours watching my father under the hood, I barely knew how to change a tire. One day while cruising through the city in my car, I began to smell burnt oil. It didn't take a genius to know that something was wrong. I pulled into the nearest oil shop, and the mechanic told me I was only a few miles from locking my engine. He asked, "When was the last time you changed or checked your oil?" I embarrassingly shrugged my shoulders. I hadn't given the oil much thought until the car began to break down. In similar ways, many of us don't give our self-care much thought until our life begins to fall apart. The mechanic shared with me that I would never have to worry about the oil running low, or my engine burning up, if I just took a little time out every few months to get it changed.

TRUTH INSIGHT

The difference between people who survive and those who thrive is proactive care, not reactive response.

CHALLENGE

Today, write out, to the best of your ability, what you do for self-care. Would you describe your current state as thriving or surviving? What changes are needed to your routine? What outside assistance do you need?

REFLECTION

_____

_____

_____

_____

_____

_____

_____

_____

_____

_____

_____

_____

SELF-DISCIPLINE

24
___
HRS

"Let food be thy medicine and medicine be thy food."
- Hippocrates

Am I the only one who really loves sweet treats? No, I mean really loves sweet treats. At one time, I had a specific cupcake shop I'd visit two to three times a week. I knew it was becoming somewhat of an addiction when my wife gave me a weekly budget for cupcakes. I had a routine. Go to work. Stop for coffee. Stop and grab a few cupcakes to decompress from stress. It was all good until I needed to buy a bigger belt and pants. The old ones, for some strange reason, were becoming skinny jeans. I was married with kids and wasn't playing sports anymore, so did it really matter? Yes. I realized I'd allowed myself to live with a lack of discipline, especially with food. Just because I wasn't "overweight" didn't mean I was feeding my body the nutrients it needed to thrive. Though the people who loved me could encourage me, it was up to me to actually follow through when no one was looking.

TRUTH INSIGHT

Changing habits can be tough, but it can happen one day at a time.

CHALLENGE

For the next 24 hours eat vegan, vegetarian, or no-carb/no-sugar. If you're unfamiliar with the terms, spend time researching what each means. *If you're under medical care, speak with your doctor before attempting this challenge.

REFLECTION

_____

_____

_____

_____

_____

_____

_____

_____

_____

_____

_____

_____

_____

_____

ORDERLY

30	30
MIN	MIN

"Clear your stuff.
Clear your mind."
- Eric M. Riddle

In school, I was the kid who, whenever he opened his backpack, had mountains of crumpled paper, worn folders, and pencils fall out. My dorm room in college was no different. It may have looked messy to others, but I managed to create a system out of that mess. Worn folders were for class work, pencils were for math, and crumbled papers were either scratch paper, test reviews, projects, or homework. It didn't start out like that, but I guess over time, things kept piling and piling, and the more I noticed, the more I'd put it off for later. The first time my wife offered to help me organize my room, I admitted to her that I was hit with a cool breeze of confidence and clarity. Why? I imagine it is because organizing clutter allows us to breathe better, effectively navigate our space, and maximize our comfort.

TRUTH INSIGHT

Clutter can overwhelm our senses and make us feel stressed; clearing clutter lessens our stress.

CHALLENGE

Today, clean, declutter, or organize something that you've noticed needs some attention, but that you've kept putting off.

REFLECTION

_____

_____

_____

_____

_____

_____

_____

_____

_____

_____

_____

_____

_____

_____

_____

_____

_____

_____

SPEAK UP

<table>
<tr><td>30
MIN</td></tr>
</table>

"To be loved but not known is comforting but superficial. To be known and not loved is our greatest fear. But to be fully known and truly loved is, well, a lot like being loved by God. It is what we need more than anything. It liberates us from pretense, humbles us out of our self-righteousness, and fortifies us for any difficulty life can throw at us."
- Timothy Keller

Have you ever had a dream that seemed so real you didn't know you were dreaming until you woke up? I've had plenty. Most of my dreams are random. You know, I'm kinda flying around having conversations with people, drinking green tea. Not sure if that means I need to buy green tea stock, but you get the picture. Occasionally though, I'll have a nightmare. I remember once having a nightmare about some creature chasing me all over the world, and every time I'd try to scream for help, I couldn't. I literally ran all over the world filled with deep fear and anxiety, but no way of expressing my thoughts or heart to anyone. That's what made it horrifying - I knew what I was feeling, but no one else around me knew, because I couldn't share. I've realized that, like my dream, many men are living a nightmare merely because they feel something - fears, needs, or excitements - but no one else knows.

TRUTH INSIGHT

Though sharing our needs, fears, and excitements can be scary, its return is invaluable.

CHALLENGE

Today, write out your fears, needs, and excitements then share them with a close friend or family member. It may be scary, but it will be well worth it.

REFLECTION

_____

_____

_____

_____

_____

_____

_____

_____

_____

_____

_____

_____

_____

PUSH IT

"You learn something valuable from all of the significant events and people, but you never touch your true potential until you challenge yourself to go beyond imposed limitations."
- Roy T. Bennett

I've seen a tremendous change in my physical and emotional health ever since starting a consistent workout routine. This wasn't always the case, but I had to make up my mind that consistent workouts needed to become a non-negotiable in my life. Even though I consistently exercise, it's easy to fall victim to doing the same exercises over and over, which results in not getting the most out of my routine. But adding variety is a useful tool to maximize your workouts.

TRUTH INSIGHT
Adding variety causes muscle confusion and increases the benefits of regular exercise.

CHALLENGE

Today, whether it's your first day back exercising or you're a regular, add a new challenging 30-minute exercise routine. If you're unsure what to do, look up routines online you'd like to try. Move at a manageable pace, but make sure you get the most out of the routine. *Always consult with your medical physician if you're under medical care or watch.

REFLECTION

_____

_____

_____

_____

_____

_____

_____

_____

_____

_____

_____

_____

_____

4 QUARTERS

30	10
MIN	$

"Most people spend more time planning a vacation than they do planning a life."
- Chet Holmes

A few years ago, I played in a teachers-versus-students basketball game at a local elementary school. Yes, you read that right - along with other adults, I suited up in a basketball jersey to demolish a group of sixth-grade boys. The first two quarters the adults were dominating the court, but by the third quarter, it was clear that these sixth-grade boys had much more energy and stamina. When the clock hit zero, the boys had won by four points. Why? Most of the adults were ready to play, but few were prepared to run the full court for four quarters. I think we do something similar when it comes to our health. Many of us seem to start off with a great pace, but over time, our health begins to wane. Perhaps we've practiced little to no intentionality when it comes to consuming a healthy amount of vitamins and minerals. We assume a strong start will mean a strong finish.

TRUTH INSIGHT

Over time, whatever ways we've failed to plan for our health will show as our body ages.

CHALLENGE

What are some natural vitamins or minerals you know your body needs but you've neglected? If you're unsure, research what vitamins and/or minerals are appropriate for your age and body type. Then, today, take a trip to the grocery store, or maybe just your kitchen, and get what you need.

REFLECTION

_____

_____

_____

_____

_____

_____

_____

_____

_____

_____

_____

_____

_____

_____

_____

BUILD IT

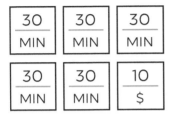

"He who works with his hands is a laborer.
He who works with his hands and his head is a craftsman.
He who works with his hands and his head and his heart is an artist."
- Francis of Assisi

There's always something that needs to be done around my house. I'm married, so when I'm unaware, my spouse makes it clear. Whether it's cleaning gutters, doing lawn care, moving furniture, or merely adding shelving to create more storage space - there's always something. Initially, it overwhelmed me that my home needed such ongoing care, but, in retrospect, it's now rewarding to know that I've done something small to add to the peace of my residence.

TRUTH INSIGHT
Investing the time and money to care well for your home can have several positive effects.

CHALLENGE

What's a small project around the house that would slightly improve the quality of your living space? It can be as simple as putting up shelving, assembling a cabinet, hanging a shoe rack, or putting together a storage bin. Today, scan your residence, determine a budget, make a plan, and, in the following days, complete a small project to add peace to your home.

REFLECTION

_____

_____

_____

_____

_____

_____

_____

_____

_____

_____

_____

_____

_____

_____

_____

DRINK UP

24
HRS

"Drinking water is essential to a healthy lifestyle."
- Stephen Curry

If I'm honest, I know I don't drink enough water. It's not that I don't believe it's vital; it's because I typically have coffee flowing through my veins. The benefits of drinking water are actually nothing less than extraordinary! An interesting fact is that around 60% of our body is comprised of water. Yes, you read that right! More than half of what's flowing under our skin is water! The benefits of drinking water range from improved skin, lower blood pressure, higher brain functionality, increased weight loss, and on and on the list of benefits goes. But despite water being accessible (and often free) in most places in the world, many people, myself included, miss the benefits of this essential body agent, solely because we haven't developed a daily routine that ensures we consume enough water.

TRUTH INSIGHT
Proper hydration is key to our bodies functioning properly.

CHALLENGE

How's your water intake? Is it a habit or inconsistent? Today, if
you're not already, drink the recommended amount of water for
your body size. Continue this challenge for the following 2 days
as well. Depending on your daily water intake, you may need to
create a plan to make sure you get enough water.

REFLECTION

_____

_____

_____

_____

_____

_____

_____

_____

_____

_____

_____

_____

_____

_____

_____

_____

_____

_____

_____

_____

_____

_____

_____

_____

_____

_____

_____

_____

_____

_____

_____

_____

_____

BUILDING ME

30	30	30
MIN	MIN	MIN

"If excellence is one of your values, not only will you self-critique and evaluate your performance consistently, you will beg others for honest feedback."
- Assegid Habtewold

There's a vast difference between being self-aware and being self-conscious. According to the dictionary, being self-aware is having knowledge of one's own character and feelings, while being self-conscious is defined as having an undue or excessive awareness of one's appearance or actions. Don't miss that. Being self-aware focuses on knowing who we are and how we feel, but self-consciousness focuses on how we look. Being self-conscious grows our insecurity, but learning to be more self-aware increases our confidence. Regardless of who you are or where you fall on the self-awareness spectrum, with a little practice, anyone can learn to be more self-aware. But it often takes some outside perspective to help us see ourselves a little clearer.

TRUTH INSIGHT

There are several benefits to being self-aware, from more internal peace to improved relationships.

CHALLENGE

Today, to help you practice self-awareness, schedule three 15-minute video chats or meetings with people you believe know and care for you. Ask them to share with you what they think are the greatest strengths and weaknesses you've displayed over the past year. If they ask for a reason, tell them you're trying to grow in self-awareness.

REFLECTION

_____

_____

_____

_____

_____

_____

_____

_____

_____

_____

_____

DATE NIGHT

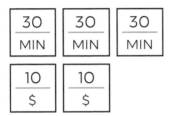

"Take time to do what makes your soul happy."
- Unknown

One of the most powerful things I've learned in recent years is that taking care of me allows me to serve others better. This doesn't magically happen. It requires that I take inventory of how I feel, identify what I need, and create a plan to make it happen. It then requires me to carve out time and actually execute that plan, without feeling guilty. So many of us feel bad for occasionally treating ourselves to things that we enjoy. But the ability to pause and do things that we love gives us the energy we need to love others. Many of us need to, literally, take ourselves on a date!

TRUTH INSIGHT
Taking care of me allows me to better care for and serve others.

CHALLENGE

Today, plan a self-care date night. Feel free to go alone or invite a friend, family member, or your mate. Dress up. Shave or style your hair, unless you're bald, in which case just shine up. Eat your favorite meal. Do an activity that energizes you. Eat your favorite sweet. Turn your phone on airplane mode. Take a picture and, if you're on social media, post it with the hashtags #Datenight #31daygrowthchallenge.

REFLECTION

_____

_____

_____

_____

_____

_____

_____

_____

_____

_____

_____

_____

_____

I FORGIVE YOU

> *"The weak can never forgive. Forgiveness is the attribute of the strong."*
> *- Mahatma Gandhi*

In 2006, I began a journey to reconnect with my father. Though he raised me and loved my mother and siblings as best as he could, there was a noticeable strain in our relationship. At the time, it would have been described as a relationship of compliance. Shortly before I left for college, we had a huge argument. I was so angry with my dad that I decided I would not speak to him unless he spoke to me first.

This silence went on for a few months into my college career, and then one day we spoke on the phone, just to patch things up. Though we'd talked, I could still feel a deep sense of disconnect with my father. It wasn't until I was married, with one child, that I realized not forgiving my father made it difficult for me to be a father. The disconnect haunted me. My father, the man who raised me, and I weren't even on good speaking terms, but I needed to communicate with him. How could I say what needed to be said without getting lost in my anger? I decided I needed to write a letter. This was by far the hardest letter I'd ever written, but forgiving my father freed me to love my daughter and others.

TRUTH INSIGHT

Without forgiveness, relationships will cease to be fully healthy.

CHALLENGE

This may be the hardest thing you've ever done, but it will free you to love with more depth. Today, write a letter to someone you need to forgive and the reasons you'd like to forgive them. This could be a parent, family member, sibling, mate, or even yourself.

REFLECTION

_____

_____

_____

_____

_____

_____

_____

_____

_____

_____

_____

_____

_____

_____

_____

_____

_____

_____

_____

_____

_____

_____

_____

_____

_____

_____

_____

_____

_____

_____

_____

_____

OTHERS

I'M GRATEFUL

> *"Let us be grateful to the people who make us happy; they are the charming gardeners who make our souls blossom."*
> - *Marcel Proust*

I love a great game of laser tag. I'm not sure if it's the clunky guns, sweaty vest, or strangers strategizing together to crush the opposing team, but I have a weird infatuation with the game. The first time I played, once we were in the play area, I noticed what seemed to be an army of lint or hair all over my hands and face. I kept cool at first, but my OCD wouldn't let me walk around with all of that lint on me. Each time I brushed it off, there was always more there. I kept asking myself, *Where did all of this lint come from? Didn't I take a shower today?*

You see, it wasn't that the lint magically appeared, it was that the black light made manifest what was already there. Like a laser tag black light, gratitude shines on relationships and makes visible what is not always so easily seen. I think many of us take expressing gratitude for granted because we believe what we feel is apparent to the other person.

TRUTH INSIGHT

Expressing gratitude not only encourages others, but it brings joy.

CHALLENGE

Today, write down a list of 10 people you're grateful for. Send them a text, private message, or email explaining why you're thankful for them.

REFLECTION

_____

_____

_____

_____

_____

_____

_____

_____

_____

_____

_____

_____

_____

JUST BECAUSE

30	10
MIN	$

"Help others without any reason and give without the expectation of receiving anything in return."
- Roy T. Bennett

I believe I'm a decently self-sufficient person. As long as I have a set routine and know exactly what it is I'd like to accomplish, I feel the need for little to no outside affirmation or attention. It wasn't until I got married to Vanja that my view on self-sufficiency began to be radically challenged. My self-sufficient attitude, though helpful for a specific task, created a lack of attentiveness towards my mate. I thought to myself, *If I'm okay, then she is too.* I distinctly remember my wife looking at me after a small argument and saying, "I feel like you don't pay attention to me." At first, I was offended, but then I realized she was right. I'd developed a pattern of only paying attention when something was big - events like birthdays and major holidays—but nothing more.

So one day I went to the grocery store, bought my wife's favorite candy, brought it home, and had it laying on the counter for her. When she saw it, she immediately lit up! At that moment I realized it's not the big things that convey attentiveness; it's the small things that say, "You matter to me."

TRUTH INSIGHT

Genuine connection is built by our responses in the big and little things.

CHALLENGE

Today, make a list of 3-5 people you care about. For each person, come up with 1-2 small ways you can be attentive to them. What's a little snack, gift, or treat you can give them? When they ask for a reason, reply, "Just because."

REFLECTION

_____

_____

_____

_____

_____

_____

_____

_____

_____

_____

_____

_____

INTERCESSION

Therefore, confess your sins to one another and pray for one another, that you may be healed. The prayer of a righteous person has great power as it is working.
James 5:16

I grew up in the era of cartoon heroes like Batman, Spider-Man, Aquaman, and many others. (I'm getting excited just thinking about this.) One of my favorite characters growing up by far was Superman. He had laser eyes, super strength, hurricane-like breath, and he could fly! Superman was almost invincible, except when he was close to Kryptonite! Unlike Superman, we're all weak, despite what we believe about ourselves. It only takes simple life circumstances to reveal that we're much less powerful than we'd like to think. This can be a hard truth to swallow, especially for those of us who go to great lengths to minimize our weaknesses. But it's in this weakness that prayer is most effective.

TRUTH INSIGHT

When we pray, we merely acknowledge before God that we are insufficient without His help. Weakness is the key to experiencing power in prayer.

CHALLENGE

Today, write down a list of 10 friends and family members you'd like to pray for. If you're unsure exactly what to pray on their behalf, ask them, "How can I pray for you?" Spend 30 minutes to an hour praying on their behalf.

REFLECTION

_____

_____

_____

_____

_____

_____

_____

_____

_____

_____

_____

_____

_____

_____

EVALUATION

"Great leaders get people to admit the truth because they know that dreams are buried under the lies they tell themselves."
- Shannon L. Alder

Have you ever been on a cruise? A few years ago my wife and I took a four-day cruise with a group of friends. It was amazing, complete with all the food you could eat, drinks you could drink, and comedy you could watch. One day I stood on the balcony and looked at the water. I looked in all directions to see if I could spot land - there was none in sight. It was amazing how small our ship seemed in the vastness of the water. With no sign of land anywhere, I realized that I had no markers to help me determine the direction of the ship. I, merely a passenger, was being carried to wherever the ship was going. Though we weren't lost, I felt lost because I really wasn't sure where we were and where we were headed. At that moment I realized how easy it was to get lost without a clear sense of purpose or direction. The same is true for relationships. Without a clear understanding of purpose or direction, relationships become confusing and hindering, not helpful. Because relationships entail a sense of interconnectedness, their goal is to create growth.

TRUTH INSIGHT

When we fail to define the direction or purpose of a relationship, we fail to get what's meant for us in it.

CHALLENGE

Today, take some time to write out a list of your friends and the reason why you are friends. Who do you need to connect with more? Why? Who do you need to add to that list? Who no longer needs to be on the list? Look over this list and attempt to build some weekly routines that help you connect consistently.

REFLECTION

_____

_____

_____

_____

_____

_____

_____

_____

_____

_____

_____

_____

PURGE

"In all things I have shown you that by working hard in this way we must help the weak and remember the words of the Lord Jesus, how he himself said, 'It is more blessed to give than to receive.'"
Acts 20:35

I love to eat - seriously. I am a vegan now and can destroy some cauliflower tacos. Before becoming a vegan, I loved going to buffets. You know, the kind of places where you stack your plate with so much food you have to grab one to two additional plates, just to make sure it doesn't slide off. There's nothing like finally sitting at the table with your three plates piled high, when, halfway through the first plate you realize you got too much food. And then, when the server comes by, you end up having her remove the second and third plates, still full of food, because you've had enough. I've realized that, when there's an abundance of resources or options, it's hard to know that we have enough. And many times not realizing we have enough causes us to be wasteful with things that others could use to improve their lives.

TRUTH INSIGHT

Giving helps loosen the grip personal greed has on our lives.

CHALLENGE

Today, go through your clothes and shoes and find the items that you barely wear or no longer wear. Give them away to charity or a person in need. What are the things you rarely use that could drastically improve the life of another person?

REFLECTION

———————————————————————

———————————————————————

———————————————————————

———————————————————————

———————————————————————

———————————————————————

———————————————————————

———————————————————————

———————————————————————

———————————————————————

———————————————————————

———————————————————————

———————————————————————

———————————————————————

AIRPLANE

30	30
MIN	MIN

> "The present moment is filled with joy and happiness. If you are attentive, you will see it."
> - Thich Nhat Hanh

With today's growing smartphone phenomenon, it's easy to be constantly glued to a screen. Many days I'll roll out of bed, notice several missed texts, emails, and social media notifications, and immediately feel the urge to read and respond to each one before talking to my mate. (Don't act like I'm the only one.) Though these notifications alert me to missed information, they can also keep me from being present with the people I love and care about. Recently, I took my family out to dinner and decided to leave my phone in the car, so I'd be more fully present. We laughed, told stories, and enjoyed a meal like we hadn't in years. I'm learning that being present without continually checking my notifications, allows my relationships to be strengthened in ways I could have never imagined.

TRUTH INSIGHT

Being present means intentionally minimizing our distractions.

CHALLENGE

Today, spend time with your mate, family, or friends; put your
phone on airplane mode or leave it in another room.

REFLECTION

_____

_____

_____

_____

_____

_____

_____

_____

_____

_____

_____

_____

_____

_____

_____

SORRY

"Apologizing does not always mean you're wrong and the other person is right. It just means you value your relationship more than your ego."
- Mark Matthews

Relationships can be very challenging, especially when you've hurt or been hurt by someone. I find that when I've done or said something hurtful to someone, I wait for them to bring it up. If time passes and they don't say anything further, I move on as if nothing happened. But, deep down, I know I've said or done something that I need to acknowledge or confess to the other person. It's like a little tug inside of me whispering, *You need to apologize.* Not long ago I had an incident with one of my sons. I knew I'd responded to him more out of anger than love and concern. After arguing with myself for a few hours, I finally sat down with him on the bed and uttered those two healing words - "I'm sorry." As soon as the words left my lips my son was visibly relieved. Though we had pretty much gotten back to normal before my apology, saying "I'm sorry" acknowledged an unspoken incident between us.

TRUTH INSIGHT

Though unprompted apologies can be difficult, they have the power to strengthen and heal our relationships.

CHALLENGE

Today, think of something you've yet to apologize for in the present or past. Even if there's nothing obviously wrong, talk with the person and ask for forgiveness.

REFLECTION

_____

_____

_____

_____

_____

_____

_____

_____

_____

_____

_____

_____

BUILD UP

30	30
MIN	MIN

> *"Affirmations are our mental vitamins, providing the supplementary positive thoughts we need to balance the barrage of negative events and thoughts we experience daily."*
> - Tia Walker

Have you ever seen the demolition of a large building? It's a sight to be seen. The workers spend weeks creating an explosives plan and, within a matter of seconds, these massive structures are reduced to a pile of ash and gravel. But comparatively, the building that took weeks to demolish took years to build. Why? It's easier to tear something down than to build something up. This is true with people. I've realized that it's easier to tear people down than it is to build them up. Tearing people down takes brashness and inconsideration, but building them up requires gentleness and significant consideration.

TRUTH INSIGHT

Building others up is contagious. When we slow down to build others up, we can create a culture around us that intends to build us up as well, not tear us down.

CHALLENGE

Today, write down 1-2 people you would like to build up. What are some things you see in them that they may not see in themselves? What are some ways you've seen their gifts, beyond their knowledge, inspire others? Call or meet with them and share the things on your list.

REFLECTION

_____

_____

_____

_____

_____

_____

_____

_____

_____

_____

_____

_____

_____

_____

HELPING HAND

30		30
MIN		MIN

As each has received a gift, use it to serve one another, as good stewards of God's varied grace.
1 Peter 4:10

One day as I was heading into the grocery store to buy lunch, I noticed an older woman with two small children. She was struggling to get them into the car. The older child was buckled into the shopping basket, while the baby sat in a car seat "goo goo gahing." At first, I was speed-walking into the store to grab a few items, but then I found myself slowing down and walking over to this woman. I asked politely, "Ma'am, can I help you put these babies into the car?" Her eyes lit up as she took a deep breath and said, "Yes please!" I lifted the toddler into the car seat and asked if I could assist with the groceries too. She looked at me as if I was an angel - a much-needed source of help that came out of nowhere. You see, everyone up to this point had walked past this woman, but I was the only one who took note of the fact that she needed a little help. Many times people in our lives could benefit from a bit of assistance, but it requires us to slow down just a tad to serve them, without being explicitly asked.

TRUTH INSIGHT

Serving others reminds us that people are important and causes relationships to flourish.

CHALLENGE

Today, what are some tangible but straightforward ways you can serve your mate, family, or friend? Ask permission first, but do it without prompting. If they attempt to give you something in return, graciously let them know there is no need.

REFLECTION

_____

_____

_____

_____

_____

_____

_____

_____

_____

_____

_____

_____

_____

_____

_____

CHECK-IN

| 30 MIN | 30 MIN |

"It's one of the blessings of old friends that you can afford to be stupid with them."
- Ralph Waldo Emerson

One of the most challenging aspects of marriage is having another person move your items to a space unknown, in the name of "organizing." I can't tell you how many headphones, socks, and articles of clothing I've lost contact with at my house because they were moved without my knowledge. But occasionally something will happen, and that item will magically reappear. Y'all, it's like Christmas! Before that Christmas-like day, after enough time has passed, I will have forgotten the thing is even lost; but once I lay eyes on it again, I'm quickly reminded of its value to me. The same is true for relationships. Sometimes, for various reasons, we lose touch with people but realize the moment we see or hear from them again how valuable they are to us.

TRUTH INSIGHT

Many relationships don't lose value over time, they lose value because we've failed to stay in contact.

CHALLENGE

Who are some valuable people that you've lost contact with over time? Today, message, call, or video chat them and share what's happening in your life now. What are some memories you cherish with them? Ask them to catch you up from when you last spoke.

REFLECTION

_____

_____

_____

_____

_____

_____

_____

_____

_____

_____

_____

_____

_____

_____

CPSIA information can be obtained
at www.ICGtesting.com
Printed in the USA
FSHW020034031218